Clinch River

The jasper of revelation is not the dull opaque stone we know today.

-William Orr

Clinch River

Susan Hankla

groundhog
POETRY PRESS

2017

Copyright © Susan Hankla 2017

All rights reserved

Library of Congress Control Number: 2017939665

ISBN: 978-0-9976766-5-5

Printed in the United States

Published by

Groundhog Poetry Press LLC
6915 Ardmore Drive
Roanoke, Virginia 24019-4403
www.groundhogpoetrypress.com

The groundhog logo is the registered trademark ™ of Groundhog Poetry Press LLC.

For Jack

CONTENTS

The Sweater, 1

Vergie Profitt, 3

Chopping Wood Before School, 4

Miss Reed, 5

Pomander, 7

The Boy in the Red Shirt, 8

The Woman Canning Dirt in Sterilized Mason Jars, 9

If You Believe on Him, You Will Not Need Fire Insurance, 10

Blue Horse, 12

After While, 13

Psalm, 14

Society for the Completion of the Road, 15

Thorn Trees, 17

How I Know Glenda, 18

To Get Back *Here*, You'll Have to, 20

Leveler, 21

Blue Tea, 22

Since My Father's Crash, 25

Small Town, 27

Ferryman, 28

Playing Alone, 30

Froot Loops, 31

The Widow, 33

Senior Will, 34

Mermaid, 36

At the New School, 37

Glenda's Mother, 38

Everyone was innocent, 39

The Silence in My Pocketbook, 41

The Man with the Pipe, 42

Shalimar, 44

Abandoned House, 45

Jesus, like an old boyfriend, 46

November, 47

Jack Tale, 48

Broom, 49

Studying the Furniture, 50

Teabag Bleeding in My Cup, 51

Lock, 52

Chance Favors the Prepared Mind, 54

Dear Husband, 55

The Dress that Never Wears Out, 57

Knock, 58

Painter of Snow Scenes, 59

Steel Cutouts on the Hill, 61

Domestications, 63

Apologia, 64

Lard, 66

Lilacs, 67

Grass Widow, 69

Giving the Ghost, 71

Subtraction, 72

Never humans, 73

Rake, 74

Sunflower, 75

Tomorrow, 76

Errata, 78

My Ghost, 80

The Sweater

She didn't see the sweater on her back
unravelling as she walked away from home,
didn't know its cables
snagged on winter's thorns
so scarletly,
delighting squirrels and magpies.

Didn't know this shredding sweater
was her shining raiment,
didn't know she'd grip its last pearl buttons
to barter for milk, for bread.

Didn't know how hard she'd have to work graveyard
in the store of winter long johns
or that she'd see the one red pair
swinging on its hanger, like a quadriplegic soldier,
like a clothespin dolly on the line from girlhood.

Or that in buckets of wash water she'd see herself,
and that she couldn't stop moving, flying
back through the years,

until the tree of her sweater's remains

rained down apples,

at first rotten, then merely bruised,

and then, finally, she tray-packed Golden Delicious,

standing in line

with others at the orchard.

Vergie Profitt

Junior's father's silence,
when he drove us with the top down—

smell of clean, sweated upon,
yellowing white wool of Junior's borrowed jacket—

thinking of it, with that boy's sweet smell
still in my nostrils—

I would know it again,
anywhere,
I swear.

That night in a dream, I saw her.
Then in the morning, read
how Vergie Profitt and her boyfriend
tilted into the Clinch, how he clawed
deeper into the drowning car
to escape being drafted.

Chopping Wood Before School

It's going to be hard to write in cursive from this day on.

You have lopped off the tip of your finger.

Almost more than anyone could handle, seeing that blood on the ax.

But no worse than the number two pencil of agony later,

when you fail to inscribe your note to Glenda,

to say how only her blue glasses with stars

see that your boots don't fit.

She who laments your accident, splits shoe leather for you

with her father's knife,

then forgets,

moves on.

But her mercy is snow that covers everything —

such divinity. Her abandoned house takes years

to be eaten by kudzu. When you come back from a war,

having mastered the trigger,

you hack through those vine monsters,

and move into the charred remains, where The Veteran,

it will be said, once poked the fire with wooden crutches,

until he blazed. "I like my own cooking,

even if it burns," he said.

Miss Reed

Personally responsible
for sharping out the offending word at the only library,
a clapboard salt box, where you could imagine
previous owners.

Books let you know former tenants, too,
if you could read the yellow card you signed.
The card got you entrance
to where the *goddamns* once lived.
You turned pages with open windows
cut in them.

Reed, prize-winning educator,
showed her children
the lynching photo,
for our good.
Said the Ku Klux Klan
met with a dragon
and scourged the town.

But some of us thought *black*
meant who came home to wash,

after laboring. Men with lamps on their heads,
hacking coal.

And their shacks had mica eyes and some, brown paper,
hastily-greased.
Don't let the cold out— Haha.
Smell of sour hog, and dirty dog.

My man's a coal-burning furnace,
when he loves.
See these purple tea bags,
this shiner.

Pomander

1.

Pushing clove spikes into thick skin,

my fingers ache. I roll the orange in cardamom,

dress it in bride's tulle,

tie it with hair ribbons.

2.

Once I saw a movie in which a Cardinal

kept an orange close to his nose

so he wouldn't have to smell the faithful.

3.

Nicking myself under an arm,

didn't burn nearly as much as my face,

my hand waving in the air, answering

the teacher's question,

seeing the bloody sleeve.

The Boy in the Red Shirt

The principal's messenger
hands our teacher the roster of scores,

then plods back across gravel and dirt.

And into the trash of pencil dust
and blackening fruit skins,

go our IQ test results.

"What did it say?" Glenda yells from the window.
"Don't know," calls the boy. "Can't read."

"Marry me," yells Glenda.

The Woman Canning Dirt in Sterilized Mason Jars

has more hope than I do.

I would have canned it, too,

had there been those stretchy

pink and russet worms to watch,

like science.

Her dirt was terrible-dry, not holy by burrow.

The dirt my mother canned could not be just any. No.

It couldn't come from hookworm plots

where the dogs lolled. She had to take a bus

to the far rough edges of county—

to a forgotten graveyard, where her people

lay down in their satin.

That was Indian dirt she canned.

And after it cured in dark ground,

she'd dig it up toward the end of the month

to make cookies

we'd eat

when we were down to Crisco

and ketchup.

If You Believe on Him, You Will Not Need Fire Insurance

My God is bigger than yours. My sheets are whiter.

Life is my china pattern. Death is my charger.

Jesus my change.

These goblets are grails.

The Tupperware burps His Name.

In your coffin be sure there is a pillow with a clean sham,

not one that is soiled from a previous occupant.

Be sure the flowers are fresh.

At the wake do not serve a seafood buffet—

it stinks like the dead, day by day.

This TP is not 2-ply, Lord.

The soap has expired, blessed be.

Good Listener, the tub butter is at a low level.

These melons are not firm, rescue me.

It was three for one dollar on TV, thank you Savior.

Is this your subtotal, Dark Angel?

The tea bags are without strings, blessed be.

The cereal is banned, have mercy.

The caplets are tampered with, Holy Co-pay.

Mildew is on the corn.

I am the responsible party. I am the man.

God is my purchase on this villa.

I empower Him the stew and my acreage.

Jesus is Lord of the Waffles.

God gives good chase in these fries.

Let the record show I was open.

God is my franchise.

He has the Mileage, blessed be.

Blue Horse

Opening the pack of blue-lined paper,
Why a blue horse? wonders Glenda.

The eyes of who I love. Yes.
This pen contains peacock blue.

Then suddenly a blue horse
gallops through the school,
wearing her mother's clothesline,
her papa chasing after it,
her stepmother running after him
fast as she can
calling,
"Stop him,
Goddamn it."

After While

Junior has to lose the baby alligator
his parents brought him back from Florida.

Then this morning, he wants to break up.
Says I'm not saved. *What?*

One slip up in his truck makes him fumbling righteous now.

Nonsense. I tried to feed it, but it just snapped at air.
And it bit me. See. Its teeth are pinking shears.

Yeah, well, I brung him.
says Junior, stripping gears.

We tip Tupperware and commend this green baby
to the stream—

watch him thrash, sink
into the Clinch.

After while, we are *just friends*.
Baptized in nose plugs,

Junior thinks he'll die, losing sin.
No one in a holler swims.

Psalm

Lord, are you the dinner bell, ringing the hill?
The closeness of birds come flying here?
Are you the sky, Lord, so blue plastic,
that's charmed me? Made my life here?

I don't mind the screaming of the gospel-singing radio—
those scriptures of spring cleaning, erasing cold
from cornices, a melted bucketful
to mop the floor, get at old salt,
tracked in from wet road.

I'll sing the song that's part breath, part coffee.
I'll be that bluebird that creaks on russet hinges outside the door,
that pecks at the suet bell on the ground.

Society for the Completion of the Road

High above Maytag, Little Miss Sunbeam's
on her billboard swing.
Her gingham trails back and forth
through coal furnace ashes—

but today she's agreed to come down from there;
sit quietly by the pencil sharpener
in this tribunal after school,
while we settle this business of "The Sticks".

We're here to set the record straight
regarding the razor strop beatings.
Regarding guilt after sex,

and how the world began,
and why those on the side of science
never raised their hands.

Ours was once a ground that pushed up boulders,
with tufts of cloud above thorn trees.
Then, tack, tack, tack, migrating swallows happy on the porch,

pecked at fleas.

Angels mightn't've wanted to swig spirits with us,

but they liked our cars.

Swarovski crystals in pitch were the stars.

Someone with a house of nice things

can't keep them anymore,

she's moving to a smaller world.

Someone decides to take the short cut home.

Grandpa's germ-cot doused in kerosene—

oh, what a blaze.

He's going to where the hangman lives,

in the margin of a composition page.

He's scrawled pretty words from his old workbook:

Thomas Time Moves On.

Were you out walking where this world suddenly ends?

Thorn Trees

You wear his father's Army shirt
and with so much pressure to please,
you've absently consented to the "4-F Club":
french,
fondle,
fumble,
fuck—

and you wonder where your cloud-folks went
and if you'll ever divine what they mean:
man with pipe,
horse,
dragon,
mermaid.
And worried, clairvoyant,
you see your little life,
and your father,
in bourbon.

How I Know Glenda

At school I touch her clammy hand, then give her

the bag of vitamins the town pharmacist, my father,

says to take her. And I see that one eye has a black dot,

where a BB's lodged, that her brother shot, missing a grouse.

Take it to my grave, not enough vow of silence for her,

so the next day I give her the whole sack of circus peanuts,

and the next day, *Hostess* snowball twins, like a pink padded bra,

and the next day potted ham on wheat,

and the next day, mayonnaise with banana on *Wonder,*

and the next day, *Lays* barbeques, and answers to the quiz,

and the next day, the dyed chick, Blue Boy,

and two newborn mice who choked on dust bunnies,

and my blue birthstone ring,

and my one-year diary and the key,

and the keys to Daddy's Grand Prix,

and to our house, at 306 Tank Hill,

and the black sheep in our basement from the barter,

and fish net stockings,

and one dozen *Piggly Wiggly* brownies, boxed, with lard icing,

and my miniature horse with English saddle,

and bikini panties embroidered with wolves' lolling tongues, and the pleather parka,

and my *Life*, with Picasso cover,

all covered in mac and please.

... to Get Back *Here*, You'll Have to

plow the patchwork's rue in your mourning dress,
and from snow and coal make a stew
of stone soup and graveyard nettles…
and build a house from paper and gall,
the spirit-wind sends crackling,
and what settles in your boots and slurs your tongue,
slithers away.
You'll have to trap and skin the rabid fox,
if you want to stay.

Now crawl out this window with your cast iron skillet
into lye-boiled November. Let your feet touch moss,
and fiddles fill your listening ears
and rock your bluing soul.
Let saws whine,
as they cut your casket from heart of pine,
that you come to sunny end.

May you come to a sunny end.

Leveler

Our teacher pushes Glenda's frostbit hands
into ice water,
Glenda screaming "Stop,"
but what's good for us often looks like it's not.

Day's spotlight
lands on red beads,
real mountain seeds,
strung onto a bib,
sewn onto Glenda's drawing
of Pocahontas.
Glenda adds breasts,
as if the Indian princess wears
a push-up bra.

Home, under lamplight,
I pore over wallet-size boyfriends,
then render them in chalky pastels,
not knowing they will someday be
frostbitten men, amputees, skeletons,

electricians, snake handlers, paratroopers,

metal workers, hunters, linemen,

coal miners, liars, laid-off fathers of fourteen,

O, Death.

Blue Tea

He beheaded sunflowers to scatter
on our front lawn the day we moved.
You should have seen Mom see those faces.
Cried like a sun without shine.

He mailed a letter to my new house.
The dirt-smeared envelope held seeds.
Said I'd made him like that tea,
when I poured it into hand cups.

I try to plant our secrets,
but sunflowers sprout from my mouth
that make Mom read my confessions,
and gasp.

Later, in a practice field
my friend sees him wait for me,
but when he sees me turn that way,
she says he drives away.

One night he comes back,
when I am in college.

Steps out from behind

a Rose of Sharon, that weed,

but just like in a dream,

we don't speak, so I can't tell him

all I've learned, or how I've moved

one-hundred towns away, and

so many enchantments beyond him, beyond myself,

through a vale.

Since My Father's Crash

How much easier it is to talk to her today.

She's giving gold from his teeth, "maybe worth money."
She's handing me his watch, still ticking.

Tonight owls perch on my bedposts.
One has his ring, the red stone gone.

The second releases a Luna moth—
green Carnival mask that flies into glass.

The third with its clawful of balloons
means someone's out of breath.

The fourth wears his face.

This strange golden light flying from a volcano,
now just drifting rags of orange and green in winter's sky.

The world that once concerned him will soon be gone.

While they pack his heart with yellow feathers,
he'll watch from a branch that will seem even smaller and smell

that snow is fixing to fall. When the fine-blown powder
flies against his final wall, he'll remember a parson

once taught him about redemption, about what passes
away, but he wore worry's hatchet blade.

Each day has seen different displays of the same skull and bones,
a silvered mirror that covets all. Now gauze takes on his unmistakable

form, even burned beyond statuary or stone, to a dark confetti.

Small Town

In town, the ABC has regulars:
man with stumps in *American Flyer*,
witch woman in soiled teddy bear coat,
quenching her awful thirst.

The girl eating a pawpaw after school
can't buy much of anything at the dime store,
except sour apple lip-gloss and taffy bacon.
Her parents have the money.

Down on the corner, at Rexall, where her father
makes coal tar salve for psoriasis,
she would like to give herself to the drugstore cowboy,
because to cat-eye glasses he looks fine.
Makes her feel less like walking away,
though he never says *stay*.

Ferryman

When you enter the lunchroom,
you accept that you will eat
fried bologna with rubbery corn bread
and soup beans with hominy,

and that you'll savor
enhancers you don't see at home—bowl
of white sugar with ketchup bottle,
a still life on the saw horse table.

You see through blue glasses,
a star at each hinge—stars that promise
the advent of change, and think you are
the only girl in elementary school
already bleeding.

Scars on both knees
are the beginnings
of cloudy whites on white
you'll cover with knee socks,
then hose.

The autograph hound

collects the names

of everyone you'll need to forget.

They smear ballpoint pen—

their faulty characters.

Playing Alone

They lay together long enough for the Goodyear Blimp
to travel the sky. By the time it disappeared,
they'd covered themselves with the peacock chenille.

But they left something in your private woods
of thorn trees—two indentations,
like ghosts of Pompeii.

Every day you prayed for a boyfriend,
tried to hold him in your compact's mirror,
tattooed his name with your father's pen,
only bending the nib.

Froot Loops

She didn't know she'd misbehaved.
School seemed so cool—you just mistrust its thrust
and gravitate to what you lack
and what you lack is freedom's smack—
pursuing boys to heart's max.

She didn't know when trying
for the loop on one boy's shirt,
she'd rip a hole dead center on his back
to show the blood-dotted undershirt
adhering to his dirty nape.

But she might have looked around
at the tatters,
at mountain shacks with souring laundry
hung on cold clotheslines,
and smelled sharp b. o.
wafting through the hot school.

Teachers in penny hairnets held no sway.
Harried, they did not love.

So she got away every day,

each day leaned into books,

till their covers became

doors.

The Widow

knew the plumber's children.

They left behind a toy in her willow tree

that didn't show up until winter, when her husband died:

a spaceman on a leafless branch, like a protective idol.

That family clearing the basement

for her move to something smaller

could have been the musicians

from Bremen, forming one line to carry those moldy things:

the slow child with fingers sliced by mower blade,

his mom, her wrist in a sling, who leaned

against the Cherokee man, so quiet he could not be seen,

and that very old man, who didn't look like he could lift a thing.

Somehow they cleared out everything,

except the piano with the Beatle figurines.

They could not heft it up her slope of yard,

even as a team.

When it was time to say goodbye

she hugged the leaf and lawn man

inherited from her spouse.

Senior Will

I give you (je donne), my love (mon amour),
I give you (je donne), all I have left behind:

children by the side of the road (les enfants),
with buckets of fishing worms (buckets of worms),
the town manager scolding his daughter
never to phone Johnny Angel. (Operator, j'ai vraiment besoin…)

I did not want to leave behind
the skinned pheasant in the freezer
shot by Grandfather, then given to Mother,
thinking she'd use that carcass to make her own hat.

Not when who I did not plan to ever leave,
stood in the dooryard, pointing
at pointy-toed kitten pumps,
saying *way, way too sexy, those.*

Is that why I covet you,
covet you,
covet you,
saying *stand in your window tonight.*

No longer scratching a slate tablet with chalk rock,
I write with black ink
on genuine rag.

Putting fingers into the bullet holes
on your legs, and arms...

Among thorn trees and sheep
and boulders,
I write your name.

Mermaid

Mirror, where is my beauty at?

Once I found kin in Cookie Lowry,
change child of Lou, *PhD*.
But Lou, the Latin teacher,
tried to mow down Daddy,
scraping ice off his Grand Prix.
(*Amo*, a mess, a matter for the sheriff.)

The art teacher calls his model,
The Information, and in a cat's cradle
of string bikini, a lifeguard badge
on her hip, Cookie straddles a chair.

Oh brackish mirror,
where is anyone's beauty at?

At the New School

She missed those girls
who beat up on girls,
and pulled out thick hanks of weedy hair
as they roiled on oiled floors.
She missed their fun.

In the distance the hills were saying goodbye
in puffball smoke,
in chalk rock sighs,
watching her fate

then gone.

Her first night, she stared into corn on a china plate
minutes after grasping her father before he dove away,
as she had when he'd thrown her to the biggest wave
to teach her to cry.

Glenda's Mother

Look in Bundy Jewelers' window,
that old-fashioned ring with two stones—

one tiny and black, a speck,
but that's it.

And what looks faceted,
like a trapped

rainbow,
is his zircon girlfriend,

drawing Papa's eyes
away from my bashful

mother, who'd be
not what you'd expect—

the diamond,
sized by *Band-Aid*.

Everyone was innocent

yet Someone dragged her frayed sleeve through the butter,
leaving grease spots on the cloth,
and Someone spit treacle into a hundred-year-old
linen napkin.

You were invited as an afterthought, because someone else
fell indisposed. You were our charity —
how we extended ourselves.

We expected you to be null, to sit still.

Yet you tracked in poop from the sodden meadow you had to cross
to get to this fine house
from yours.

And you offered your hosts daisies, plebe and sooty, dripping
to the floor.

You're the one who turned the conversation toward yourself,
didn't you. You're who talked out of turn, then lost the thread.

You sent the anonymous letter.

Stole the silver.

Smoked in the shed.

Fucked the wait staff.

Ate the eggs. Then you wriggled into two,

and each half ran in opposite directions,

oozing all over our nice world,

didn't you?

The Silence in My Pocketbook

The palm reader in the dark corner of the restaurant lays out her cards.

A boy wears nose plugs in the Clinch, and is baptized, right where he drowned the souvenir alligator.

The girl who thought squiggles on her *Hostess* cake bore meaning, sits writing in a café.

Is there no one who does not want to be saved?

Find in the oil drum, the stillborn.

Blood in the ice for years, where the girl's skate flew to part her streaming hair.

Why does worry work so hard to erase beauty?
Women with shiners pack pomegranates.

The Man with The Pipe

He's Mr. Lonely,
too;

a kind of Messiah
with a horn of fire.

The Man with the Pipe
makes a house call,

and finds you home,
brings his bag load of unnatural sops.

"Trick or Treat," he slurs.

He lists by the door
making you recite names of the dead

already jotted, like tattoos,
on his arm:

Catherine Eddowes,
Elizabeth Stride,

Mary Ann Nichols,
Mary Jane Kelly,
Annie Chapman…

as if he would have you study

for your final
breath.

> *For the victims of Jack the Ripper's heinous crimes against women,*
> *Whitechapel Rd., 1888*

Shalimar

Magazine picture bride with the sun on a pendant
around her glistening neck. You can smell
the scent sample in the page's gutter.
Her dress dripping artificial dew;
crown on her head, mirror tiara—
a shattered something—
rainbow edge,
light-crease,
chink and clink of a wild dream
to come into being in *Bride* magazine.

In an opposite place, in an Opposite,
this dress drips *Clorox* wash water,
filmy, used bath water,
all kinds of natural wet,
the sun's sweat diamonds—
a rag to catch mine.
Crown of thorns, and my face
in the bucket
of gleaming parings,
well water carried,
the magazine in my hands shines.

Abandoned House

The black fence lying in the snowdrift forms the iron sentence,
Country house condemned,
its row of swords sheathed in snow.

A windowpane catches gold.
It's four o'clock in the evening.
Is this where loneliness tries to live,

but then looks out two gleaming squares
to be instantly contained by sun?
It must be the hottest house,

the flint of February rubbing March—
what bedding wouldn't blaze?
That's why snow needs to hug the roof,

dripping in to calm the drapes
crying into armchairs.

Jesus, like an old boyfriend

a girl's just broken up with,

the one no one can ever have,

he's so handsome.

But Abraham Lincoln is much harder to adopt,

because the War of Northern Aggression

is still being fought in the lunchroom.

Witness the Cain and Abel of it all,

knocking the stuffing out of each other,

and the mean girls throwing rocks

at the new girl. Me.

November

The snout's red,
throat cut
to bleed the meat.

On the outdoor table,
the centered grin.

Once you have seen
a beheading,

you will never again
collect decorative baskets.

Now the body's upside down
strung from the clothesline
boiled neat,

and field hands scrape
bristling hairs
in the sleet.

Jack Tale

Someone's in this bodice ripper,

a slattern of mercy with her jar of glowworms—
night's child,
bagatelle, eluding almshouse,
selling twists of auburn hair.

Five-sided absinthe glass,
yellow-green and half-full
of icebergs and caves
and consciousness, with striped brown wings
and dark red dreams.

Lily-white hand,
when you lean on the player piano,
I hear you sing of Slag Group, Inc.

Pinch prick of Whitechapel Rd.,
in grass-stained panties,
what's your life's expectancy?

Broom

Standing on your head,
you lean in one corner,
listening to frying
in my black pan.

What else have you heard?

You've swept things under
the hooked rug for years,
because dust is your business.

You've lent me your straws
to test the doneness of cakes,
dipped blonde strands into the batter,

the direction of your tresses
dictated by the way you lean,

listening.

Studying the Furniture

First that big mistake with his handsaw,
trying to make the baby's crib,
then that gash across one corner of the table we ate at,
where, from then on, I could not set down a heavy dish.

And in my yellow chair, where I sat still chewing,
my hand found deeper cuts on one side,
where his hand slipped
making something else never finished —

a perfectly good, pretty chair that will forever snag hose.

If only I had studied more,
gotten down on the floor with my big belly,
I would have found more jagged marks,

all around the doors.

Teabag Bleeding in My Cup

I send my husband to make tea
while I question angels,
but I have to tell him
where the bags are, and
please use hotter water.

I just can't make it today.
Last time while it steeped,
I sat by this window
watching the frozen field,
wondering: *Am I out of time?*
then closed the ball-fringed drapes,
my tea mug stone.

But the strings on the bags
tag rooms that we've been happy in,
where someone left a Mason jar
that held a broken wing.

"*Drink your tea,*" is a towhee
mocking me.

I don't know how many times I've drunk this.

Lock

Vivid red hair

Just one strand

Hold to it like the kite's tail

Turn in winter glare

So red and golden

Pulling you somewhere

to woven-hair jewelry of the departed,

who speak through hairpins hidden in the wall.

Better than a phone call.

Can't say as I remember who that one is.

Looks like one of theirs maybe, but then again

Wasn't she the one ran across the grass, then gave away all her candy?

Wasn't she by the creek gave some self in the hollows of sleep?

Wasn't she to whom the creek sang, "Ta-ta, to your intactness"?

Wasn't she stupidly numb to the smoothing out of all sharp rocks in the burbling,

now she was missing a membrane?

(Why does spreading the jambes haunt one?)

Then she hung her marked bloomers on the clothesline for all to see,

her poverty flag.

Who then rocked this one? Don't exactly recall. Heard she sat beneath the thorn tree, rocking herself rightly, possessed.

Her little fingers bled on autumn's pages,

leaving no address.

Chance Favors the Prepared Mind

Glenda is well informed by *Glamour*.
August's features *Verushka* as a college freshman.
With kohl-rimmed eyes and frosted bangs,
V. models the fur jacket that catches Glenda's eye.
That's what I'll need if I want to go to college.
In his lay-offs, can Glenda's papa do that much trapping?
She must have that silver fox.
In the lunchroom Glenda consults the *Hostess* cupcake oracle,
to see what she'll wear.

Dear Husband,

I am writing you this letter,
because I've left town
in order to get away from you
so that I can write a letter to you
since you have never received a letter from me,
your wife, and I think it is time.

My writing to you is not as easy
as my system of hanging your clothes.
Even though one sentence is penned
and closely followed by the next in a line
broken only by punctuation,
I don't know today what I hang out to dry.

I am leaving behind a clothesline of washed pants.
They will be frozen in tomorrow's frost,
and you will let them thaw and sun bleach
and maybe the birds will find your pockets,
as I did.

Every pie baked, I dropped,
but you ate of them. You drank

from the chipped glass,

shard in your mouth.

You have carried me as a soldier carries one photo.

In squelching mud.

In soot and ash.

Through the slights of a life.

That photo doesn't change.

But how does time get by with running away so recklessly?

After you read this,

set by the creek, and watch small wingings

rise where they must go.

The Dress That Never Wears Out

Glenda stands on the needlepoint stool
turning, testing the evenness of the hem
of the finished garment.

A car drives up the road and its lights
blind her as she turns to face the window
she has made a mirror.

All day at her Singer,
she's worked the treadle barefoot
making a grass green dress,

belted with python, caught and cured—
gift from her bridge partner

at the V. A. Hospital—
dreamer of dyslexic nightmares,
cured and caught.

Knock

When you were her child,

she wrote one letter to you at camp.

It included all the angles of her focus:

who died,

who might die,

what burned,

what was torn down.

You thought of how often you waited in her front yard

after school, when she didn't hear your knocking.

And of her not watering the philodendron.

At Christmas, she would stake it,

tie a vibrant ornament on the stick,

as if.

Painter of Snow Scenes

I was going to the dance, but it was canceled.
I spent three hours preparing
and I would have submitted—
I'd shaved my legs for that—
should it happen, finally.

I wore a hand-knitted sweater,
green and ribbed and stylish, now unseen.
And I sat inside the warm house,
disappointed and tired.

With him it would have been first footprints
in snow, and we would hear
whispers of ice
on the windshield as we drove.
Something being born in quiet.

Pitch now. Lamps lit.
The year disappears.
When it was still orange and crimson,
and the fir tree held that burning sun,

and its laden branches lifted white loads to heaven,

I thought I was going to wear stockings and dance,
and that my legs would be smooth as glass.

Steel Cut-outs on the Hill

The insane welder made these steel four:

Man with Pipe is the judge and he's rigid—
grim cutout, he's darkening doors.

Stallion gives chase to Man with Pipe.
Give sweet grass to Eros, when Stallion wins.

Dragon guards Victorian gold.
They must get past him.

But Mermaid will dive through snake water.
Hear her fiddle cry?

Man with Pipe rides Stallion.
First he charges through a terrible war.

Singeing them is Dragon,
but they must get to *Her*.

Mermaid holds a mirror that has lost silver.
Shows five little motherless girls.

She brings up gold from grandmother's finger.
Dragon says, "Put that back."

On Stallion, Man with Pipe charges Dragon.
They all fall in.

The family Bible tugs Mermaid's hair
so she can't swim.

Now they're all at the bottom of the manmade lake
in the flooded house.

Plant rosemary on their graves,
and remember what is past.

Domestications

Left on the shelf with her mother,

Glenda collects shells.

Visits the outlet store,

searches through botched monograms

for *I.H.S* in the bin.

Beyond the weight of towels,

copperheads coil

under armchairs at home.

Glenda can see how her mother thinks—

witches' work.

Her mother, who tied jingle bells to her baby shoes,

so she could tell *who it was coming into her rooms*.

All doors unhinged and stacked in the shed,

she dragged the straight razor

across bracelets of skin.

Glenda buys a purple towel

to hold her mother in.

Apologia

…if I had known when I heard the knocking
and opened the door to the lady begging alms,
that all at my back was even then fading
and that was the Plan.

…if I had not been stretched by a stretch of road
from Clinch to Big Lick.
If I had not been suspended,
stretched, to there. If I hadn't viewed poverty from a car.
If I had known my own.

…if I had not worn that binding panty girdle, lest I be penetrated,
if I had not wanted to be pretty.
A pretty life.
So pretty.

…if I had let life kiss me, oh anywhere.
And if I had only seen that I am no more
than that rock that holds papers in place…

…if I had known the heart-broken Jesus, or the blue-robed Mary, or that the Plan is just like using us as teabags.

Had I known my mother's pure heart and my father's open one.

If I had known anything of value, even who that was
who invented the rote of writing one hundred times
"I must not talk in class." Even that.
That, even. Exactly that.

Or had I been just your personal teabag,
dipped one hundred times,
turning back into plain water.

Had my life not had such distance, been held at arm's length,
by such a trying distance.

…if I had lived at the top of a hill and not at the bottom,
might have read the sky,
might have known money was never good here.
Might have fallen into your arms,
and, God forbid, stayed.

Lard

streaked with pink capillaries

slid down a frying pan in her friend's kitchen.

She saw the big buckets in sagging rows

on *Deskins'* shelves, and knew

all the town's mothers had bag boys hauling

those heavy, fatted cans to their cars, too,

so the frying could go on.

Who could she tell of that carnage in cook stoves?

And how to get clear of everyday catastrophes —

the paraplegic veteran, a cursing Lazarus,

soiling newspapers in *Deskins'* parking lot?

She scotch taped

Art Treasures of the Louvre

scenes into the New Testament.

Then *Clubfoot Boy*

shouldered country ham,

and Bruegel's beggars

crawled on stumps

across familiar land.

Lilacs

in the field,

that field, flat field

with wisteria that snakes up the green tree

blue wisteria

that drips down in May

same one that in December shoots its seed—

well, how can that same field look

empty and promising

depending on the day—

same field

cluttered, but then, too gone?

How do you know how to look empty,

but not be it,

with the fullness that says you will empty,

that same flower which in December shoots its seed

from a brown husk once blue perfume? (How does it do it?)

And how can it be that just yesterday, only yesterday,

I was full, but today, empty

as never before?

And someone right next to me,
says, "I came here to photograph that house
with the purple squares,
only because it had right next to it
such lovely purple trees,
you call them *lilacs*, I believe,
yes, *lilacs*, right next to it,
all matching,
but today, where did they go?"

Grass Widow

The day you don't come home intact
I'm drawing cold water

to wash my hair, and as the bucket
bumps bottomless, a voice wells

from a black rainbow. It says
He can't pay the bills.

Reeling in the weight of that,
pulley taut, I slosh some out.

I bring up not enough.
Tie a scarf around my head.

Do without. And you come back.
Say I keep a dirty house.

Move yourself permanently outside,
scry clouds while I burn trash.

From the porch you read the sky,
say you see battle scenes

of Moses and the Philistines.

Say you see clouds chock-full of *deads;*

you spend your days naming them.

Then by and by, my wishing well

takes a drink.

Giving the Ghost

Where are the blue horses, the ones not bearing
the notes I never wrote you?

Save me from waking to this cavalry of night.
I know you do not stumble into this waste of the slain.

You are smoke with no name.
Were you ever beaten—not by the Opponent,

who is Worthy, but by your father?
I was, I wanted to say, but you showed me

the empty socket, where your brother missed the grouse.
Your eyes should be green as summers in the Clinch.

You said you like the algae, how its murk protects the wiggle tails.
Tadpoles, you explained, that turn into frogs,

like a fairytale.

Subtraction

Not one mark on the red coat, but when she takes it off,
a small hole shows in her shirt, like a cigarette burn,
then stings when she pushes up the sleeve,
seeing strings of skin.
Falling, catching on one elbow,
whole front flat to the road,
gravel in knees through pant legs,
just taking a walk.

It hurts to sleep. She smells wood smoke, tastes ghosts.
Something about this beyond the ruin of her flesh.
A body gets the news first.

All through that New Year's,
a family massacred—nothing personal—

and last thing,
the mother still conscious that morning
before closing her eyes,
sees her two babies and husband
lifting up to God.

For Kathryn Harvey and Family, in memory, murdered together, 2006

Never Humans

just animals during hunting season—

a couple of dogs going at a raccoon,

or deer eating jonquils at the edge of road.

Hear that mocking bird of my mother?

See my re-buttoned pink troublemaker?

I've touched the human tar of your hands.

Rake

I once stacked sticks beneath that tree
that has since dropped its branches in an ice storm,
so there's really no time to start over.
Winter's here. At first unofficially,
in spitting snows.
I could try to personalize that falling—
stop and remember being kissed,
but leaves will fall,
and me hanging on,
and that last dangling one,
animated by the force no one sees.

I once raked leaves
when I was angry with my mother
and now that memory rakes me.

Sunflower

Her copper hair cross-boned with bobby pins,
Glenda pries the lid of the *Eight O'Clock* coffee tin
where she keeps the sunflower's face,
to see it's more like a heart now.
Wearing crinoline under plaid at school,
she was the tallest.
One eye a cracked marble, she sat in the back row
facing away, watching Junior take his blade to history,
slicing out the pages.

Tomorrow

A summer dusk and you're walking, seeking air,
when you see a mission's neon cross,

at first unaware of the sign, "Clean, Used Cars",
and the men in lawn chairs.

They pass a bottle back and forth, and joke —
flick lit smokes, just missing your ghost.

The wives work in thrift stores
across from their children, playing on porches —

swelter in rooms of polyester threads.
Your years are one long hour, languishing

with the one you didn't wed,
his sweet *aubade* — honey in a biscuit.

Tourist, what wouldn't you give to cut
your losses here in a motel room?

What else will arise as you walk past the mannequin
that advertises a yard sale "tomorrow, behind Sears"?

The mission's cross glows more brightly, as flames bank,
and indigo bruises the sky—Cassiopeia in her chair,

beaten by Orion's belt. You think of the boy
who brought chicken to school

to cook on the radiator, each day to savor
what was in that steaming foil,

with a whole red bottle of ketchup—

how he knew joy.

Errata

The box of school papers she's saved
just to see her mother's name on each report card
so freshly written, as if the years have not passed.

Then Glenda spies an old math test,
and for fun, she does the problem over—
and finds the teacher's error.

Then her erasure becomes a black hole
to view time through,
to see herself parched and near-sighted
in the back row.

People in those last seats never
did well: the boy who missed
one hundred days for hunting deer,
the pregnant girl, who drowned in the Clinch,
eloping—
others in flip flops who went without real
shoes, and herself in altered dresses.

But math, like branch water, asked nothing of her.

Math, odorless, colorless, like water

in the fountains in the hall, where she bent

down, cupping it to her lips, drinking

from that stream—

Nothing but these numbers in memory now.

She counts all her surrenders to poverty's fate—

one score finally settled at this late date.

My Ghost

Sometimes he's when ice in the glass plunks and makes sweet tea to splash out.

It stops you—he's cold like that. All over my chest,

and I think how the dead can't see.

He can't see me. (I don't know.)

I can't see him, but he's there.

"I know you're there," I say to him.

I look at the sunflower I've saved like a corsage

I'll never wear, and remember his face, full of ardor.

Recipient of things when a girl,

I wanted him to get something from me.

I sent him powder and socks for the rot—

soldier's heart, what he later got.

Not nothing to me. I didn't lump him with others who made fun.

He did me no hurt. Not like the one retched on his carved

school desk when I brushed past, smelling the cut onion of me;
no way to bathe then and shine, without breaking through

a gleamy barrier of ice on a pond. At 4 AM on the frozen skim,
I find him.

Acknowledgments

Infinite love and appreciation go to Liz Whitehurst, Brenda Barrows, Allen Gay, Derek Kannemeyer, Tricia Pearsall, Maria Butler, Twiggy Munford, Jim Metz and Amy Sheets for their insightful support.

I am indebted to the Virginia Center for the Creative Arts, for sanctuary many times over.

Also indebted to

...The Robert Frost Poetry Festival

...The Fine Arts Work Center

...Annette Lucks, who translated some poems into German

...Howard Finster, Man of Visions, in memory

...Valery Nash, in memory

Gratitude to Keith and Rosmarie Waldrop, Burning Deck Press, for publishing *I Am Running Home*.

Obliged to these publications:

Richmond Quarterly Review: "The Leveler" (in earlier form)

The Hollins Critic: "Grass Widow"

Artemis: "Lilacs", "Painter of Snow Scenes"

I hold in highest esteem cover artist Laura Pharis, who envisioned "a landscape, pregnant with snow."

Beholden to Richard Dillard, forever, plus in awe of. Thank you.

Thanks to and for my husband, Jack Glover. And to my sister, Cathy Hankla, deepest gratitude.

This book was designed and set in Palatino Linotype by RHWD Industries

Cover art by Laura Pharis

Printed by Salem Printing

groundhog
POETRY PRESS